MW01059943

# HUNTING AND GATHERING

*a comedy
about finding your place*

**BROADWAY PLAY PUBLISHING INC**
224 E 62nd St, NY NY 10065-8201
212 772-8334 fax: 212 772-8358
BroadwayPlayPubl.com

HUNTING AND GATHERING
© Copyright 2008 by Brooke Berman

All rights reserved. This work is fully protected under the copyright laws of the United States of America. No part of this publication may be photocopied, reproduced, stored in a retrieval system, or transmitted, in any form or by any means, electronic, mechanical, recording, or otherwise, without the prior permission of the publisher. Additional copies of this play are available from the publisher.

Written permission is required for live performance of any sort. This includes readings, cuttings, scenes, and excerpts. For amateur and stock performances, please contact Broadway Play Publishing Inc. For all other rights contact Seth Glewen, The Gersh Agency, 41 Madison Ave, 33rd fl, NY NY 10010.

First printing: December 2008
This printing: June 2014
I S B N: 0-88145-405-2

Book design: Marie Donovan
Word processing: Microsoft Word
Typographic controls: Ventura Publisher
Typeface: Palatino
Printed and bound in the U S A

PUBLISHED BY B P P I

HUNTING AND GATHERING
THE LIDDY PLAYS
OUT OF THE WATER
A PERFECT COUPLE
SMASHING
THE TRIPLE HAPPINESS
UNTIL WE FIND EACH OTHER

Brooke Berman is an award-winning playwright, screenwriter and memoirist whose work has been produced and published across the U S.  Originally trained as an actor and solo performer in the experimental theater, Brooke began performing her own work on the Lower East Side of Manhattan before receiving formal training in playwriting from the Juilliard School. Her play HUNTING AND GATHERING, which premiered at Primary Stages, directed by Leigh Silverman, was named one of the Ten Best of 2008 by New York Magazine.

Brooke's memoir, *No Place Like Home*, published by Random House, was released in June, 2010 and named "Highbrow/Brilliant" by New York Magazine's Approval Matrix.  The book made Elle.com's "Top Ten Summer Reads," LA Magazine's summer reading roundup and the EW piece "If You Like GIRLS, You'll Love …"

Brooke's plays include: 1300 LAFAYETTE EAST (JET), HUNTING AND GATHERING (Primary Stages, Theater 7 Chicago); SMASHING (The Play Company, The Eugene O'Neill Theater Center); UNTIL WE FIND EACH OTHER (Steppenwolf, The Eugene O'Neill Theater Center); THE TRIPLE HAPPINESS (Second Stage, The Playwrights Center,  ASK, the Hourglass Group, The Royal Court Theatre), SAM AND LUCY (SPF), A PERFECT COUPLE (WET, Naked Angels, Arielle Tepper Productions), OUT OF THE WATER (Red Stitch Theatre, Melbourne, Australia; Cape Cod Theater Project, ARS Nova, Pioneer Theater, NYU's

Tisch Lab), CASUAL ENCOUNTERS (New Dramatists Creativity Fund, Rising Phoenix Rep), THE LIDDY PLAYS (Crashbox Theater, Rising Phoenix Rep, Williamstown Theater Festival Apprentice Workshop), DANCING WITH A DEVIL (Life Under 30 @ Actors Theater of Louisville) and others. Her plays have been produced and developed across the US at theaters including: Soho Rep, Williamstown Theater Festival, Naked Angels, MCC, New Dramatists, New Georges, The Womens Project, The Humana Festival, and The Bay Area Playwrights Foundation. In the UK, her work has been developed at The Royal Court Theatre, The National Theatre Studio and Pentabus. Her plays are published by Broadway Play Publishing, Playscripts, Backstage Books and Smith & Kraus.

Brooke recently wrote and directed her first short film, UGGS FOR GAZA, based on a short story by Gordon Haber. UGGS premiered at the Aspen International ShortsFest where it won an Audience Special Recognition award. ALL SAINTS DAY, a short film she wrote directed by Will Frears, won Best Narrative Short at the Savannah Film Festival and played at the Tribeca Film Festival in 2008. She adapted her play SMASHING for Natalie Portman and has written features for The Mark Gordon Company, Vox Films, Red Crown, and Fugitive Films.

Brooke is the recipient of a Berilla Kerr Award, a Helen Merrill Award, two Francesca Primus Awards, two LeCompte du Nuoy awards and a commissioning grant from the National Foundation for Jewish Culture. She completed a seven-year residency at New Dramatists, where she served on the Board of Directors and developed countless plays. She has received support for her work from the MacDowell Colony and the Corporation of Yaddo and commissions from Arielle Tepper Productions and C T C in Minneapolis.

Brooke has taught as a guest artist in the New York City public school system and at colleges including Eugene Lang, Fordham, and Barnard, as well as privately through the "24 With 5 Teaching Collective" which she co-created at New Dramatists. She spent five years as the Director of the Playwrights Unit for M C C Theater's Youth Company, a free after-school program for N Y C youth. She has mentored with the Young Storytellers Foundation in Los Angeles and Young Playwrights in New York.

Brooke attended Barnard College and is a graduate of The Juilliard School. She is a member of the Dramatists Guild, PEN and the M C C Playwrights Coalition.

More information: www.brookeberman.net

HUNTING AND GATHERING was first produced
by Primary Stages (Casey Childs, Executive producer;
Andrew Leynse, Artistic Director; Elliot Fox, Managing
Director) with its first public performance on 22
January 2008. The cast and creative contributors were:

RUTH............................................................ Keira Naughton
ASTOR ...................................................... Michael Chernus
JESSE............................................................ Jeremy Shamos
BESS.......................................................... Mamie Gummer

Director....................................................Leigh Silverman
Set design ........................................................David Korins
Costume design ....................................... Miranda Hoffman
Lighting design ..................................................Ben Stanton
Original music & sound design............... Robert Kaplowitz
Production stage manager ....................................Kate Hefel
Production supervisor.............................P R F Productions
Casting ..................................... Stephanie Klapper Casting
Press representative ...............................................O & M Co
Director of development.....................................Erica Raven
Director of marketing.........................................Shanta Mali
Associate artistic director ............................ Michelle Bossy


The play was developed through the M C C Theater
Playwrights Coalition, New Dramatists, and
Underwood Theater Company, with special thanks to
Mandy Hackett, Emily Morse, Josh Hecht, and Daryl
Roth.

# CHARACTERS & SETTING

RUTH, *early thirties*
ASTOR, *mid to late twenties*
JESSE, *thirty-five*
BESS, *twenty*

*New York City, present-day*

# NOTES

It's important that this play move like a coherent
collage, a coherent, interwoven whole. Scene breaks are
not meant to isolate any one "scene" or "monologue"
or "sequence" and hence, they are noted as such.
Each element should roll into the next, the new scene
crashing in, demanding to be heard. The monologues
are direct-address—bright, clear, and to the point. The
characters are smart and think fast.

As far as design, it's entirely possible that these
characters carry their worlds on their back or contain
pieces that roll/unroll/pack up/get stored. Be careful
of not overloading the text with design fabulousness—
language is the musical score.

(RUTH)

RUTH: This is a list of all the apartments in which I
have lived in the past fifteen years that I have been
alone, I mean, an adult:
*(She begins the list.)*
340 East 9th Street
117 East 7th Street.
600 Bergen
101 Thompson
45 Pierrepont
309 East 9th,
258 West 72nd
66 West 9th
27 First Avenue
A month in Trump Plaza with that girl from Argentina
274 West 19th (The roommate who forgot to mention
he was in debt to the landlord. So. Evicted. Then…),
131 Fifth Avenue (Brooklyn)
Four months in San Francisco:
22nd St. between Mission and South Van Ness, 2242
Union, squatting in graduate housing at Stanford—
"Escondido Village"—
A drive up the West coast to Seattle, Portland,
Back to New York:
25 Fifth Avenue
A month in Vermont
636 Washington
118 North 11th St (Brooklyn)
431 16th St (Brooklyn)
680 Manhattan Avenue (Brooklyn)

Back to Manhattan:
345 West Broadway
205 West 103rd
Two weeks on Rivington, six weeks out of town, a
week on a friend's sofa-bed, six weeks at 428 East 9th—
that writer—
And now, here, this:
A housesit.
For someone very kind.
Someone out of town. Someone I recently kissed.
Someone entirely different from Jesse.
(Jesse who said "this is a beginning" but was married
to someone else…)
But that was a year ago.
Fully behind me.
And here I am today in this apartment in Queens.
Because someone new said the magic word:
Stay.
He said, Stay.

*(The Housing Fugue)*

RUTH: HOUSESIT. A housesit is where you sit in
someone's house while they're away. You get their
mail, water their plants, make sure no one breaks
in, and in exchange they let you live there, usually
without paying rent, because paying rent would make
it a "sublet". House-sitting and subletting both involve
reading all of their books and copying their C Ds—
sometimes eating their food, but mostly not. It's more
a cultural exercise than a culinary one. I have been
"house-sitting" for the last year. My friend Astor has
been "couch-surfing" just as long.

*(ASTOR joins her on stage:)*

ASTOR: COUCH SURF. Couch surfing is when you stay
with people for free and sleep on the couch. It is called
"couch surfing" because you're riding a wave. You

can't stay with any one person long enough for them to
get sick of you. You have to keep moving and ride with
the times. For instance if one of them suddenly breaks
up with their boyfriend and needs you to go away, or
falls in love with you, or if someone suddenly has a
cousin visiting from California, you may have to get off
of their couch. Plus, and this isn't like, I mean I know
it sounds crass, but you're always looking for a better
situation. You are always sniffing out the place where
you can stay without being in anyone's way at all. This
can go on for months, really. You don't intend for it to,
but it can if need be. If the need needs be. My friend
Dave, he's that guy who moved above the porn store
in Harlem—he doesn't go out too much anymore—but
anyway, he lived like this, marginally, for a few years.
I think it was bad. I think it messed him up. He kept on
being marginal for like, a lot longer than a person can.

(JESSE *joins the others on stage.*)

ASTOR: My brother Jesse has never been marginal.

JESSE: I was always the person who moved in. Never
the person who looked. When I was in college, I lived
in the dorms. When we moved off-campus, someone
else found the place. When I moved in with my wife,
she already had a place. When we wanted a bigger
place, she went out and found it. I don't even know
how. I don't know how she did many of the things she
did. I think she has a gift. And so, when I needed to
find an apartment by myself, I had to seek help.
REAL ESTATE AGENTS.
Brokers. In New York City, these people are entitled
to fifteen percent of the total rent, and yet, the only
thing they have to do to earn that money is have keys
to the apartment and show it to you. They don't stay
involved. Even when you secretly wish they would.
They show you the places, give you the paperwork and

take a cut. Not all real estate agents are blood-sucking parasites. Some are quite nice.

The broker who showed me *this* place was motherly. I trusted her. She said, "Jesse, I'm telling you, take this place. You're not gonna find better," —and I believed her. I could tell she cared. I prefer female brokers to male. I believe they have some interest in whether I find the right home, how I get settled, how I will unpack and what to do if the plumbing breaks. Or whatever it is that plumbing does. I don't actually know very much about "plumbing".

ASTOR: CRAIG'S LIST. A website dedicated to helping people connect. I have this/ you need this/ I want that/ you have that/ let's email and meet. You can surf craigslist every single day. You can spend enough time on the site that you notice each fluctuation and catch every new post as it appears. I have been on craigslist A LOT.

RUTH: THE CLASSIFIEDS. Apartment shares. You: Depressed, cat-owning vegetarian seeking invisible stranger to eliminate half the rent while leaving no trace, no dent, no impact and no scars. Single White Female remembers scary movies about psychopaths with good haircuts. Seeking someone clean who will do no damage and pay things on time. Me: Lovely single female, also vegetarian, not always single, but single right now, maybe, or maybe waiting for someone to come home. But, here's me, lovely and smart, moving a lot, very dynamic. Ruth without Naomi: wither thou goest, I will go, anyhow, me this Person seeking home. Long-term, short-term okay, sublet okay, own room a must, own room with door and window too and ideally a closet, a nice closet. I have read Virginia Woolf, and I need a room of my own. With a door, a window and a closet. Under a thousand dollars. In Manhattan. Close to subway.

ASTOR: Two bedrooms, three bedrooms, need roommates. Can't afford to live alone, need roommates. Good roommates, the right roommates, roommates who are clean but who won't be freaked out if I'm not clean. Roommates I want to come home to. Who like to cook on Sunday mornings but not too early and sit up on the roof late at night with a six-pack or two. A twelve. And some whiskey. And cigarettes. And the stars. Getting wiser. Cuz the weird thing about living with people is how you really live with them, you get to know them, you rely on them and they become part of you in some way that defies any of the words we currently use for who those people are.

*(To the fugue, add* BESS, *a pretty twenty year-old girl, separate from the others on stage.)*

BESS: Dear Mom and Dad,
School is great. I'm learning a lot. I've moved out of the dorms and into a house in Brooklyn with six other girls, but it's okay. We mostly all have our own rooms except for Lucy who doesn't need one because she has a boyfriend. I hope to be in Manhattan by summer. Otherwise, not much else to tell. Classes are fine. Glad you liked Paris. Thanks for the chocolate.
Love,
Bess

*(End of fugue. Shift into:)*

*(*JESSE's *new apartment. A one-bedroom.* ASTOR, *his brother, helps him move in.)*

ASTOR: It's great.

JESSE: It's small.

ASTOR: Efficient. You have an extra bedroom.

JESSE: My office.

ASTOR: It looks like a second bedroom.

JESSE: But I'm using it as an office.

ASTOR: Gotcha.

JESSE: There's something so final about moving. The
search is over! The movers dropped my things off this
morning and left, and I thought, is this what it comes
down to? These boxes. The table. The rug. Deirdre
got everything else—the apartment, all the rest of the
furniture, our furniture. I got the table and the rug.

ASTOR: So? You got the table and the rug. And an extra
bedroom. Make a list of shit you need. Mom always
told me to do that first.

JESSE: Mom never told me that. What shit do I need?

ASTOR: Windex. Garbage bags. Incense?

JESSE: No incense.

ASTOR: Okay. No incense. Lightbulbs.

(JESSE *starts making a list.*)

JESSE: It's temporary.

ASTOR: Everything's temporary.

JESSE: In a year, I'm going to find something and buy.
You should think about that. It's a buyer's market.
Everyone says. Why waste your money on rent
when you can own? The market supports it, and
you could probably find something in one of those
neighborhoods you live in.

ASTOR: What neighborhoods I live in? The ones I can
afford?

JESSE: The market supports buying. And some of those
neighborhoods have deals. That's all I'm saying.

ASTOR: The market supports my asshole.

JESSE: Meaning?

ASTOR: Meaning, it just cracks me up when people are like "You should look into buying." Everyone who says that shit is either rich or knows someone rich or is married to someone rich or getting money from their parents or some combination of the above. I mean, if I don't have the credentials or money for a first and last months' rent, how do you think I'm going to get a bank loan? I mean, come on.

JESSE: I'm not getting money from Mom.

ASTOR: Well that's good because I couldn't even be in contact with you anymore if you were. Our whole adult sibling whatever you want to call it friendship or whatever, adult brother rapport—

JESSE: We've worked on that rapport.

ASTOR: Whatever. It would be out the window, decimated.

JESSE: Because I bought.

ASTOR: Because you were living off our mother. And not sharing your second bedroom.

JESSE: It's an office. Where are you living?

ASTOR: Oh. I can't talk about that.

JESSE: Why not?

ASTOR: Because it is too goddamned depressing, that's why not. It's just so all around dire. I'm looking for a place again, and it's—you know, looking, looking, looking.

JESSE: You should call Mom. Tell her where you're living, living, living.

ASTOR: I can't even begin to think about calling Mom so just get off my entire case about that okay? I am protecting Mom from needless worry. It's just too much to be like "Hi, Mom, it's me, and I'm here for the next ten days, and then I'm there for a week but you

can't call me there because… Blah, blah, blah, blah,
blah, Mom, blah, blah—" I mean, Come on, Man. Mom
doesn't need to hear that shit. You know what she'll
do with that shit? With my goddamned itinerary or
whatever you call it? She'll worry. That's what she'll
do. That is what moms do. They worry. It is their job
to worry, their function. It's biologically determined.
They are wired to worry so that the young don't die.

JESSE: Call her. She wants to know where you are.

ASTOR: Thanks. I'll make a note of it. Call Mom and
freak her shit out with a list of the couches I'm staying
on and why and for how long.

JESSE: You could be settled.

ASTOR: I'm settled. I'm just always in flux. Do you have
any idea how hard it is to find real estate in this City
without a regular job, without corporate sponsorship
in the form of "salary", while trying to pursue
alternative lifestyles like education, technology and
music? All of this is objectively hard, and "the market"
is competitive. So right now, for me, it's just all about
subletting and couches. But that's fine. For me, for
now.
You don't get it.

JESSE: I'm an academic.

ASTOR: You work for major institution that also
happens to own most of the real estate north of 100th
Street.

JESSE: You could get a real job.

ASTOR: I have, like, ten "real jobs". Besides, I'm
looking for something—a way of life, an experience, an
existential contract. Like Henry David Thoreau.

JESSE: Henry David Thoreau brought his laundry home
to his mother the entire time he lived on Walden Pond.
And I don't work for a corporation.

ASTOR: You work for Columbia University.

JESSE: It's a university.

ASTOR: It acts like a corporation.

JESSE: Fine.

ASTOR: Mom isn't doing my laundry.

JESSE: Fine. *(Lament, off the apartment:)* It's not where I thought I'd end up.

ASTOR: Stop that. Nothing in your situation implies "ending up". You left your wife.

JESSE: She left me.

ASTOR: Whatever.

JESSE: I cheated. With Ruth.

ASTOR: You weren't happy

JESSE: I wasn't? When I try to think of that time, or any of the times leading up to that time, it all goes blank. *(Then, re: the apartment)* Do you like the floors?

ASTOR: What do you mean blank?

JESSE: Blank.

ASTOR: Really?

JESSE: Yes. Really. Blank. Washes of color blank. Like looking at a Rothko. With this vague sense that Deirdre is looking at the Rothko with me, and she's really mad. And then, all of the sudden, I'm single and looking at apartments. Deposited on the other side of this MESS that I never really saw myself participating in, and then, then, I see myself participating and then, guilt. Just guilt. Did I mention the guilt?

ASTOR: I love the apartment. And I never liked Deirdre. Mom never liked her either. We thought she was cold.

JESSE: She's not cold. She's just from Maine.

ASTOR: *(Reaching into a box)* What the fuck are these?

JESSE: Cassette tapes.

ASTOR: Obsolete, Brother Man. Obso-lete. If you hold on to the archaic forms of preservation, you do not empower yourself to move forward.

JESSE: I like them. Are you in touch with her?

ASTOR: Mom?

JESSE: Ruth.

ASTOR: I'm in touch.

JESSE: Is she okay?

ASTOR: You know how the lotus is able to blossom even though it lives in all this mud? It thrives in a hostile environment

JESSE: She's in a hostile environment?

ASTOR: Queens.

JESSE: What's she doing in Queens?

ASTOR: I'm not entirely certain.

JESSE: She hates me. Does she hate me?

ASTOR: I'm not entirely certain. We don't talk about you.

JESSE: She should get her act together. She's a great person, but lost. Right? Like you. Right? She should, you both should—

ASTOR: I should go. I'm helping a friend move.

(Scene: ASTOR helps RUTH move into her place.)

RUTH: Thanks for helping.

ASTOR: You have no stuff.

RUTH: Most of it's in the storage space.

ASTOR: Ah, the storage space.

RUTH: I visit sometimes. Just to say hi. Like, "Hi, Stuff. How are you?" I open the metal door and pull out my one big armchair, and I sit down and look at all my stuff. It's weird. And strangely liberating. To be without stuff. The storage space has helped me enter this cocoon from which I will emerge a butterfly.

ASTOR: Cool.

RUTH: I know, right? *(Then)* How is he? You were with him, right? I can always tell.

ASTOR: Who?

*(RUTH says nothing.)*

ASTOR: He's okay.

RUTH: You know, one of the major reasons why not to sleep with someone else's spouse, besides the Bible and all that, is the way they take up psychic space in your life. And you dream about the wife.

ASTOR: You dream about Deirdre?

RUTH: Even now. Every woman over a certain age on public transportation is her. To me. Every one. I ride the bus and think, did you used to be married to the guy I used to sleep with? The one who shattered my heart into eight million pieces?

ASTOR: She doesn't ride the bus.

RUTH: Another reason: the married person does not have enough time in the day to devote to two partners. Maybe in polygamous households where this is publicly condoned, but in our society, it doesn't work. One needs too much.

ASTOR: One does.

RUTH: And people don't have that much time. And I think that's part of what the Bible was getting at anyhow. The things that are right just make more sense. The things that are wrong are harder to sustain.

ASTOR: I'm glad you're over that.

RUTH: Me too. Me too.

ASTOR: *(Changing the subject)* Queens freaks me out. People say this is a "real" neighborhood like that's supposed to mean something. Like Greek bakeries make it "real"?

RUTH: Oh come one. It's nice.

ASTOR: It isn't.

RUTH: The Museum of the Moving Image is nearby.

ASTOR: Have you been there?

RUTH: I just moved in.

ASTOR: But do you plan to go there?

RUTH: There's a sculpture park.

ASTOR: Do you plan to go there?

RUTH: I plan to go to the Greek bakeries.

ASTOR: Ah. But do you really think you will go anywhere else in the borough of Queens?

RUTH: They say it's "up and coming". And I have a job in Long Island City. An after-school program in the projects. Working with teenage girls. They're fierce. I told them not to sleep with married men too. I told them, "Girls, a man who does not give you his home phone number does not live alone!" I said, "Beware!"

ASTOR: *(Teasing)* I bet they love you.

RUTH: They do!

ASTOR: Whose place is this again?

RUTH: The Canadian. An actor. We met at the public library.

ASTOR: He sounds random.

RUTH: If you believe in that.

ASTOR: You could have stayed with me.

RUTH: Where?

ASTOR: I have an air mattress.

RUTH: Exactly

ASTOR: I'd have taken the air mattress.

RUTH: I can't stay with you. You may not know this yet, but after thirty, air mattresses are not charming.

ASTOR: Okay, old lady.

RUTH: Don't call me old. This is good. And who even knows what'll happen.

ASTOR: What'll happen?

RUTH: Who even knows. That's what I'm saying. Who even knows? This is my favorite part. Before anyone gets seriously injured.

ASTOR: Are you and he… *(?)*

RUTH: Well. I don't know. We kissed.

ASTOR: Before or after he offered his place?

RUTH: I don't remember.

ASTOR: Great.

RUTH: He calls. Late at night. For messages—

ASTOR: Romantic.

RUTH: And I call him back, and his cell phone, the one he is carrying, lights up blue. It says HOME, because I'm calling from his home number, and he says, "Hello, Home".

ASTOR: Can I vomit now?

RUTH: What if this is where I belong?

ASTOR: Sweetie. This is not where you belong.

RUTH: Have I told you about the sheets? Go. Look at the sheets. I bet they were woven by really special genetically engineered silkworms. Getting into bed is like—

ASTOR: Gross.

RUTH: No. Seriously. We have a lot in common.

ASTOR: Like the same address?

RUTH: No, no, no. We share a belief that things can be good.

*(Scene)*

BESS: Dear Mom and Dad,
Today, Lucy and her boyfriend broke up which means now she wants her own room and very suddenly has "issues" with sleeping on the futon in the living room while still paying her sixth of the rent. I think this is an existential dilemma since she agreed to the terms when we signed the lease and her inability to hold onto a man is not any of the rest of our problem. I think it's incredibly selfish to ask the rest of us to change our entire domestic arrangement just because her situation has oh so suddenly changed. I bought her a copy of that book that was on Oprah last month. I hope that she finds peace. And I don't plan on giving up my room to help her.
P S: They have this thing in Brooklyn called The Food Co-op. It sounds like a good idea only it involves this mandatory work detail, and they don't let you do it just once for the whole house, but all six of us have to take our own shift. The other girls are all about the Food Co-op, but I'd rather shop at the grocery store, pay more and not work once a month. I'm not sure how this will resolve itself. But I have no intention of showing up on a weekend to—whatever it is you do on work detail at the Food Co-op. Shelve things? Take inventory? Check people out? Oh no. This will not be happening. Park Slope is this really funny part of Brooklyn where everyone pretends they live in

Woodstock, only they don't and there are like twenty Starbucks already. It's basically a white liberal ghetto for Wesleyan grads with Asian babies. Honestly, I'm over the entire borough. It takes way too long to get anywhere and you have to act like you care about communal food. Anyway, I have to go. It takes like eight years to get into the City and I can't be late for class.

Bess

*(Scene:* JESSE *teaching.)*

JESSE: So. That's class. Read Hardy. And be prepared to talk about "The New Woman". In the Victorian novel. Bring a list of five questions about the text and one observation. Oh, and an observation should be in complete sentences and should prove that you're actually awake and reading the text. Next week, we start Austen. And that, my friends, will be fun.

*(*BESS *approaches* JESSE *after class.)*

BESS: Excuse me. Do you have a moment?

JESSE: Of course.

BESS: Are you single?

JESSE: In what sense?

BESS: The dating sense.

JESSE: Are you insane?

BESS: I'm just wondering.

JESSE: I'm recently divorced. Why?

BESS: I think you're cute.

JESSE: You do?

BESS: Strange, troubled. But cute. I thought you should know.

JESSE: What's your name?

BESS: Bess.

JESSE: Like Elizabeth?

BESS: No. Like Bess.

JESSE: I see.

BESS: I know this is highly unconventional but frankly, I'm only auditing your class not really taking it for credit, so I figured… It would be okay with me if you wanted to hang out off campus. Your class is slow, but you turn me on.

JESSE: My class is slow? *(Beat)* Do you want to go out for coffee?

BESS: No. I want to go out for whiskey. You in?

*(They leave. BESS leads, JESSE follows.)*

*(Scene: RUTH on the phone. Possibly wrapped in the ridiculously soft sheets)*

RUTH: I'm glad you called.

I know, me too, me too.

It's been a year since…well I was in this… See, I've always been very judgmental about things like "Adultery"…like it's just something you don't do. But any time I'm exceptionally judgmental about something, I find myself *doing* the very thing I say is wrong, which teaches me humility, so… Last year I was humble and fucking a married guy.

Jesse and I both thought it would be a fling. And then it wasn't a fling. And then we broke up. And now we don't speak. Ever. At all. Which I gotta say, I find SHOCKING. I thought, you know, initially I thought, if I step away, it will all work out. If I do the right thing, if I give him up…I just think, you know, if it's love, it works out. Right?

Anyway, I'm totally over it. But I wanted you to know because… I haven't been with anyone since, and…well…staying here… It's very intimate to be in someone's bed without them.

*(She giggles)*

Me too.

*(She giggles again)*

Oh. Me too.

*(She hears something disturbing. Something about a girlfriend. And she sits up, abruptly.)*

What do you mean?

Repeat that.

What do you mean, Girlfriend?

What do you mean, Open?

I don't understand.

Oh.

I understand.

Yes. Of course I understand.

No. It is totally my mistake. I take full responsibility for how it is so totally my mistake.

Yes.

Of course.

Of course.

Oh my God of course.

I can't stay here.

No, it's fine.

Really.

When are you coming home?

I see.

No. Problem.

I will just be gone.

By then.

I'll be gone.

*(She hangs up the phone)*

Fuck.

*(Scene: RUTH and ASTOR)*

ASTOR: He was random. A port in the storm. You need a revolutionary.

RUTH: I need a place to stay starting on the first.

ASTOR: Stay with me.

RUTH: I can't stay with you.

ASTOR: I'll take the air mattress. You can have The Futon.

RUTH: No, that's okay. I can find something. I have two whole weeks.

ASTOR: Do you have any money saved?

RUTH: Not enough for first month, last month, and security.

ASTOR: I love that they call it "security".

RUTH: How come all the jobs I feel I could DO aren't jobs that could actually enable me to LIVE like a person?

ASTOR: Or have health insurance.

RUTH: Health Insurance! A dream! You know, I thought this guy—

ASTOR: No, you didn't. Not really.

RUTH: Really. Okay, not really. You're right. I don't know. I wanted it to work out.

ASTOR: Work out how?

RUTH: Work out good. Like, "Follow your heart and it leads you home" good. How come it's not leading me home?

*(Scene: BESS and JESSE, a dive bar downtown)*

JESSE: This is my favorite kind of bar. It has character. History. These floors are—

BESS: Old.

JESSE: Tile. This is the kind of bar writers write about.

BESS: It isn't clean or well lit. And at night, it's really loud.

JESSE: Still. This is a Jake Bar. (The guy in the Hemingway stories.)

BESS: Yeah, I know. I'm getting another whiskey. You want anything?

(JESSE *shakes his head no—then corrects himself. Yes.* BESS *returns with drinks.*)

JESSE: It's very bold to ask out your Lit professor. Don't you think?

BESS: Maybe. But I'm just auditing. Want to make out?

JESSE: Yes.

(BESS *and* JESSE *do.*)

JESSE: I was married.

BESS: Oh?

JESSE: For a few years.

BESS: I see.

JESSE: I cheated.

BESS: Oh?

JESSE: For a few months.

BESS: Sure.

JESSE: My wife didn't know. Until much, much later.

BESS: Why are you telling me this?

JESSE: I don't know.

BESS: Your wife probably knew.

JESSE: Do you think?

BESS: Women always do. Even if we don't say anything.

(JESSE *looks busted.*)

BESS: My dad cheated on my mom, and she totally knew. She'd pretend she didn't—and it wasn't anything he did or said—she could just—sense it, smell it on him. And she never called him on it. But she told us, me and my sister. And then we knew. And then everyone knew.

JESSE: Are they still together?

BESS: Sure. Why break up a good marriage? They buy things, take trips, whatever. This part's getting dull. Want to make out again?

(JESSE *does as told.*)

*(Scene:* RUTH*)*

RUTH: This is a list of the apartments I am currently looking at:
542 East 11th Street.
430 East 9th (basement. Can I live in a basement?)
258 East 10th (also a basement)
513 East 13th—stall shower, no tub. Microwave, no stove.
154 Orchard (twice)
142 Orchard
38 Orchard (roaches)
195 Stanton (ground floor. Next to schoolyard. Some mice.)
Oh, and the place I couldn't afford on Ninth. Which, even though it was out of my price range also did not have a bathtub.
Any day now, I'm going to find something.
Any. Day. Now.

*(Scene)*

RUTH: I have news.

ASTOR: I also have news.

RUTH/ASTOR: You first.

ASTOR/RUTH: No, you.

RUTH: Okay. Do you remember when I was working at the job near the Seaport and I met that girl Ginger who was a friend of that guy from the café where I used to waitress when I was a waitress?

ASTOR: Not really.

RUTH: Well. I ran into her yesterday in Union Square and she's going out of town to start a career in Industrials—that's like, I don't know what that means but apparently it pays very well, or can, and there's a big market for it in—whatever city she comes from—but she doesn't want to give up her lease because it's a cheap rent controlled studio for under six hundred dollars in a fairly not dangerous neighborhood. And I said yes. And I'm moving in! I have a home!

ASTOR: What if she wants to come back?

RUTH: Yeah well. There are risks.

ASTOR: But Sweetie. She might get to wherever she's going and realize she is no longer capable of living there and she might not get any jobs and she might come home and want her apartment back.

RUTH: Don't be pessimistic.

ASTOR: I am being pragmatic.

RUTH: Since when are you a pragmatist?

ASTOR: Is she taking her stuff?

RUTH: I didn't ask.

ASTOR: Ask.

RUTH: Come on! It could be great!

ASTOR: Which fairly not dangerous neighborhood?

RUTH: South of Chinatown, north of the Seaport.

ASTOR: Don't they have some fancy name for that? So-Chi-To? No-Sea-Po?

RUTH: Be happy for me.

ASTOR: I just wish she were taking her stuff.

RUTH: What's your news?

ASTOR: Okay. Remember my friend Rainn? The guy who used to move art?

RUTH: The art mover.

ASTOR: Right. Well, Rainn is selling his van. And I am buying it. Right Livelihood. Not a career. Not an identity. But a kind of service, something I can offer. I'm gonna be a Man with Van.

RUTH: That's amazing!

ASTOR: And I can do all kinds of things with the van. I can use it for work, for pleasure, for sleeping, for travel. Trips. Excursions. Field trips. Road trips. Pilgrimage. Mardi Gras. All of this is within the power and scope of a Man with Van.

RUTH: Can you help me move next weekend?

ASTOR: Do you even have to ask?

*(Scene)*

BESS: Dear Mom and Dad,
Lucy is a nightmare. She is having nightmares, and she is becoming one. She stays up all night long watching T V with the sound turned up really loud, and she has developed this new habit of leaving her shoes in the bathroom. Cassie and Elena have tried talking to her, but she becomes hostile. I'm thinking of moving out. I've started seeing someone, and he's very nice. He's my lit professor, but he's young. Kind of young. He has recently gotten out of a very unhealthy relationship and I think I might be able to turn his life around and then maybe I could move in and get away from Lucy.

At least for the rest of the year before I can figure out another plan. Don't worry though. We're using birth control, and my therapist approves.

I love you.

Bess

*(Scene:* BESS *visits* JESSE's *apartment)*

BESS: You need to finish unpacking.

JESSE: I do!

BESS: You need a couch.

JESSE: I know.

BESS: Why don't you get one?

JESSE: I don't know how.

BESS: What do you mean, you don't know how?

*(*JESSE *looks bewildered and lost.)*

BESS: I'll help you. We'll go to IKEA.

*(IKEA, nexus of evil)*

JESSE: I'm going to IKEA.

ASTOR: Oh no! Dude! IKEA is the nexus of Evil. They're not selling furniture. They're selling Identity.

JESSE: Are they good identities?

BESS: It's in Elizabeth. That's New Jersey.

JESSE: I try not to go back to New Jersey. Unless I absolutely have to.

BESS: You have to.

JESSE: Okay.

*(Lights up on* RUTH, *all four actors now address the audience as they did in The Housing Fugue.)*

RUTH: This is my stuff:

ASTOR: Any mention of IKEA makes Furniture Bob quote from the Book of Revelations. About the final days.

RUTH: I got the dresser from Furniture Bob. He used to sell stuff on Lafayette Street.
The desk, from Atlantic Avenue.
The chair, from a flea market upstate.
Boxes: mostly books and notebooks. Some Polaroids. From each of my apartments.
A trunk. I got the trunk by making out with some guy who had the same birthday as me.
These things will remain here, in the Storage Space, while I go to Ginger's.

ASTOR: Furniture Bob says, "A piece of furniture is like a beautiful woman."

BESS: You want light. You want ease. You want utility. And then, you want to be able to get rid of it when you can afford something better.

ASTOR: —completely unique, an individual. Distinctive. You don't want one that looks like everyone else, mass-produced, fake boobs, straightened hair, all that.

RUTH: You want your history to be light. In case you have to carry it on your back or load it into a four by six room.

BESS: A person's furniture tells you who they are. What they value. There is some stuff you just need.

JESSE: What do I need? Can you just tell me what I need? Look. My brother started a list. But we never made it past Windex, garbage bags, and light bulbs.

BESS: A dining room table, four chairs, a kitchen table, two more chairs, and that thing you put inside the wine bottle when you take out the cork—what's that thing called?

ASTOR: The beauty of the air mattress is that it's portable. And if the place you're crashing has a bed, so much the better.

RUTH: I slept on a futon on the floor until I was thirty-two. Then I met Jesse, and he said, "You sleep on a futon on the floor?" The next day I went out and bought a bed. Now the bed lives in Storage.

JESSE: Thank God for 1-800-MATTRESS. And there are many kinds of beds. Did you know that? Hard top, soft top, pillow top…I bought the bed before I even moved in.

ASTOR: I like things that roll up. I like things that travel well. I like things that don't make you need other things.

JESSE: Then, I went to Bed, Bath and Beyond and bought sheets, four towels, and something to boil water in. The rest has been waiting. You can make great furniture by draping sheets over boxes.

BESS: Sheets over boxes doesn't work. This does not have to be scary. And then we'll have Swedish fish and lingonberry tea in the IKEA café. It'll be fun.

JESSE: Lingonberry tea?

BESS: It'll be fun.

RUTH: I have moved so much I have it down to a science. I can make anything home. A couple of books, a scented candle in a tin, some fresh flowers, and we're good. This candle is grapefruit-vanilla. What more does one need?

ASTOR: A place to meditate. If the vibe's not right in the apartment, I'll go meditate on the roof. That's really cool. Unless there's an alarm. Or bird shit.

BESS: And we can check out those cute flea markets. You know the ones I mean? They're cute.

JESSE: Okay. I'm ready. Lets do it. Take me to IKEA. And the cute flea markets. I think I can do this.

BESS: Of course you can. You just need help. We'll do basics at IKEA, then cool antique-y things for emphasis. I can't believe it's taken you this long.

JESSE: I started.

BESS: But you didn't finish. You have to finish. You're gonna feel so much better once this is done. Listen. These are the names of the IKEA furniture lines— Alvar, Applaro, Matius, Sommar, Diod. Doesn't that just sound great?

JESSE: It sounds vaguely futuristic and troubling.

BESS: And if you pay them extra, they'll come over and put it together.

JESSE: What do you mean "put it together"?

BESS: *(Leading him off)* Come on.

*(Scene: Man with van)*

ASTOR: Hey. Hi there. Hey.
I'm returning your call.
Got your message.
I want to help.
Let me help.
I charge money
But I get the job done.
You say you need your band equipment
to travel from one side of the city to another?
Easy. I do that.
Precious artwork?
I do that too.
I move those things.
I carry them.
I get them
to where they need to be.
All your things.

Everything you hold
carries energy, your charge.
Your life unfolds
according to what kind of charge
you carry—
and where
you place
that charge
and how much of it
you're willing to let go of,
Change.
That's right.
Evolve.
That's what this is all about.
E-VO-LUTION.
Let me help.
It's my business.
I get you there in one piece.
Man with Van. That's me.
The Man with The Van.
I'm the Man.
With the Van.

*(Scene)*

JESSE: I'm confused. Why are you driving a van?

ASTOR: Right livelihood.

JESSE: I don't know what that means. What happened
to computers and music?

ASTOR: Computers and music are my passion. This will
be my livelihood. My *dharma*. Or is it *bhakti*? The thing
you do that's labor and not love?

JESSE: What are you talking about?

ASTOR: Marx and the Buddha. Some weird place in my
brain where the two dance. What's that thing you do

on a retreat when you're doing selfless service, what's that called—?

JESSE: Punishment?

ASTOR: No. It's called something. It's called…oh, fuck, I can't think of what it's called.

JESSE: I'm sleeping with one of my students.

ASTOR: Really?

JESSE: It's recent. I just recently started sleeping with her. I mean, seeing her. Or, rather, seeing her outside of class. She is the one who took me, to, you know.

ASTOR: Can I meet her? Show her the van? Chicks are going to love the van.

JESSE: No.

ASTOR: Okay.

JESSE: She's shy. Fragile.

ASTOR: She might love the van. Fragile chicks love the van.

JESSE: Have you read *Tess of the D'Urbervilles*?

ASTOR: I saw the movie. *Love* that Nastassia Kinski. She's fucking hot. Did you see *Cat People*? Like, she eats this meat with her bare hands in the middle of the night, and it's like, I mean, the best commercial for being a carnivore I have ever seen. She like tears into it with her bare—

JESSE: You can't meet this girl. She's very shy. Like Tess. Soft-spoken. Long-suffering. Fragile. She needs me to protect her because she is so shy and fragile. She is not like Natassia Kinski in Cat People.

*(Scene:* BESS *is in the midst of another letter home.)*

BESS: All the girls are learning to shoot. We're also playing poker, but I think that shooting is the really essential thing. We practice on a video game called

Big Buck Hunter. We love relaxing into our lower
bodies, waiting for the moment—the one right before
the kill. "See it, then shoot it." This guy named Steve
showed me how to hold the gun right up next to my
face, between the torso and the arm, higher up, like a
violin. Remember when I learned to play violin in the
fifth grade? Remember how I sucked? Well, I do not
suck at Buck Hunter. I have a natural killer's instinct,
which I think will help me immeasurably as I work my
way through the Western European canon, A K A my
college career. Speaking of the which, I'm taking this
awesome class called "Essential Cinema of New York:
Cassevetes, Scorsese, Allen and Lee". I'm either writing
my midterm on *She's Gotta Have It* or else, *Manhattan*.
Did you guys see that one in the theaters? It's this
really cool old black and white movie about when New
York was intellectual and people still lived uptown.
Spike Lee's movie is also black and white, and people
also live uptown, but it's different. Anyway. Later
Skaters.

Bess

*(Scene: BESS and JESSE making out on his new IKEA furniture.)*

BESS: My therapist says you're mean to me because you
think all women are poisonous.

JESSE: I am not mean to you.

BESS: My therapist says you shouldn't have gotten
into a relationship at all so soon after splitting up with
Whatshername. Your wife, not that other girl.

JESSE: Deirdre. My wife.

BESS: Right. Her.

JESSE: Tell your therapist that this is a rebound
relationship. Tell him—

BESS: Her.

JESSE: Of course. Tell HER that we're on the rebound.

BESS: I'm not on the rebound. I'm fine.

JESSE: Well, I'm on the rebound.

BESS: Maybe. But you jumped in pretty fast and you can't tread water. I'm stronger than you. You'll die here. With me. So start acting a little nicer.

*(Scene:* RUTH *on the phone with* ASTOR*)*

RUTH: So okay, the super just came by. He's the green card husband of, you know, Ginger, whose apartment this is. He says there are all these dead birds and crack vials on the roof, just above my apartment, he says it looks like someone's getting fucked up and cutting the heads off of birds. He doesn't think it has anything to do with Ramona, the transsexual prostitute who lives downstairs. He thinks it is random. He thinks it is kids. He thinks we're safe. *(She takes a deep breath, glancing around and then, up…)* I don't know.

*(Sequence)*

*(*RUTH *and* JESSE*)*

*(*RUTH *and* JESSE *are seen, each in their apartment/sublet, in the middle of the night. Time seems strange. Neither can sleep. Each opens a book, then closes the book. Each turns on a computer, then walks away from it. Someone stands. Someone paces. Someone eats. Still, no sleep. Each reaches for the phone. Picks it up. Puts it back down. Someone goes to the refrigerator. Opens the refrigerator door, closes it. Each stands.)*

RUTH: I can't stay here.

JESSE: I can't stay here.

RUTH: This is not working out.

JESSE: It's not working out.

JESSE/RUTH: Mother. Fucker.

*(Scene: JESSE and ASTOR in JESSE's apartment.)*

ASTOR: What are you talking about!?

JESSE: I just have to. You work so hard to get the right apartment and then you don't even want to be in it because it's small and dark and the neighbors are loud and all of your furniture reminds you of the person you left. Or the person taking you to IKEA.

ASTOR: Oh.

JESSE: Besides, I can't sleep. I stay up all night not sleeping. I don't want to stay here. I hate being alone in this tiny rectangular shoe box with half a stove—we call this an apartment? Will you stay here? While I'm gone? Will you?

ASTOR: Well—

JESSE: And I shouldn't be sleeping with students. It's just wrong.

ASTOR: Well—

JESSE: So, stay here. Will you stay here? I really want you to. Please? Spring break. And Easter weekend. Two whole weeks.

ASTOR: Where will you go?

JESSE: North.

ASTOR: I see.

JESSE: Maybe I'll get as far as Canada.

ASTOR: You can think in Canada.

JESSE: Exactly. So will you stay? Please? I'd love knowing you were here. And, um, would it be okay, I mean, could I...?

ASTOR: Yes?

JESSE: Can I borrow the van?

*(Scene: ASTOR calls RUTH.)*

ASTOR: Okay, look. I know this is weird, but hear me out. I don't want you staying in the place with the decapitated birds. And I have this idea. See—and I know it's weird and I don't want it to be—but in terms of the greater nonattachment problem solving of our respective situations, what I'm thinking is—

*(Scene)*

BESS: In a van?

JESSE: It's my brother's.

BESS: Can I come?

JESSE: No.

BESS: Where are you going?

JESSE: Canada.

BESS: Really?

JESSE: It's not you.

BESS: Of course it's not me.

JESSE: Things are moving so fast. I have to—you're a student.

BESS: Technically.

JESSE: I just need to think. You're the first person I've been with since the divorce. And you're not even legal.

BESS: I'm legal.

JESSE: You're twenty.

BESS: That's legal.

JESSE: You know what I mean.

BESS: Come up with better reasons. Because these are dumb. Did you ever see *Manhattan*?

JESSE: Sure.

BESS: Woody Allen thinks he's being all whatever by going off with Diane Keaton, but she's really just a neurotic mess and in the end, he chooses Mariel Hemingway. He realizes she was the adult all along. And then, you know, it's Woody Allen—I don't' know why anyone was so surprised when later in his life he—

JESSE: That's not what he realizes. I don't think he realizes that Mariel Hemingway was an adult. I think he just chooses her. It's not her adulthood he's choosing.

BESS: Semantics.

JESSE: I won't be gone long.

BESS: It's fine.

JESSE: Will you be okay?

BESS: No, I'll be like totally heartbroken and starve myself into a diabetic coma. Of course I'll be okay.

(BESS *stomps off.* JESSE *goes to the van.*)

(*Scene:* RUTH *comes over to* JESSE'*s house, carrying a bag of her stuff.*)

RUTH: It's weird.

ASTOR: I know.

RUTH: Are you sure this was his idea?

ASTOR: Of course! He practically begged me to invite you over. He was happy to help you out. Just don't try to thank him, I mean, by email or phone or anything because he's—on a retreat. A Buddhist retreat. In French Canada. The kind where you do a lot of selfless service, and he can't be reached. They don't even speak English. Just Buddhist French. He took the van.

RUTH: He doesn't know.

ASTOR: That he took the van? I hope he does. He's driving the motherfucker.

RUTH: That I'm here.

ASTOR: He knows you're here.

RUTH: You're a terrible liar. As bad as me. I can't stay here.

ASTOR: Think of it as alimony. He owes you.

RUTH: He doesn't owe me.

ASTOR: Think about it as a favor to me.

RUTH: To you?

ASTOR: Yes. I need you to stay. To help me feel at home. I'm not used to all this space. And I might get scared of the dark. And I might need a friend here. I'm terrible at watering plants. They look at me and die. And I don't want to worry about you in that Ginger place with the no-headed birds. Ten days somewhere free. And clean. No decapitation, no transsexual prostitutes, no more stepping over Ginger's stuff. You're staying.

RUTH: Well—

ASTOR: Put your bags down. I'll open a bottle of wine. He has this bizarre contraption where you, you stick it in the bottle after you've taken out the cork. Like, who owns these things!?

(ASTOR *goes into the kitchen to get a bottle of wine.* RUTH *puts her stuff down, starts to investigate. She runs her fingers along the spines of* JESSE'*s books.* ASTOR *returns, catching her in the act.*)

ASTOR: Hey.

RUTH: Hey.

ASTOR: What are you doing?

RUTH: I don't know.

ASTOR: You're touching his books.

RUTH: The spines of his books.

ASTOR: I see.

RUTH: Yeah. Bad, right?

(RUTH *removes her hands from the books.* ASTOR *hands her a glass of wine.*)

ASTOR: You take the bedroom.

RUTH: Oh. No. You take the bedroom.

ASTOR: Are you sure? You were, you know, about the air mattress, so I just thought...

RUTH: I'm not sleeping in his bed.

ASTOR: You're right. I didn't think of that. Sorry.

RUTH: I'm not sleeping in his bed.

ASTOR: We can make up the couch.

RUTH: Because I'm not sleeping in his bed.

ASTOR: No problem. The couch will be great. We'll load it up with pillows. (*He goes to investigate the pillow situation.*) He's got like, a linen closet. A linen closet and that thing for the unfinished bottle of Chianti. And everything is from IKEA. I'm so glad we have different fathers. (*He returns with bedding.*)

RUTH: Remember when I lived in that loft with that guy?
His girlfriend said, "What if you two lived here forever?"

ASTOR: She was high.

RUTH: Still, though. What's "forever"? Every time I think something is "forever", I'm wrong.

ASTOR: Remember when you met me?

RUTH: You had blue hair.

ASTOR: I was living over on Delancey with those girls.

RUTH: They had blue hair too.

ASTOR: It was a ritual.

RUTH: Right. Jesse brought me over there to look at something—what was I looking at?

ASTOR: It was an art opening.

RUTH: I don't remember the art.

ASTOR: We all had blue hair.

RUTH: Oh.

ASTOR: My point is: out of all the relationships that happened that year, ours lasted. Ours. Yours with me.

RUTH: I guess you never know.

ASTOR: I knew.

*(Beat)*

RUTH: I'm gonna go out.

*(RUTH goes for her jacket. ASTOR watches.)*

ASTOR: Okay.

RUTH: Can I take a set of keys?

*(ASTOR hands them to RUTH.)*

RUTH: You want anything?

*(ASTOR nods no.)*

RUTH: Okay. Don't wait up.

*(RUTH goes. ASTOR makes up the sofa for her. He clears space for her. He sits, alone. Waiting)*

*(Scene: Big Buck Hunter)*

*(RUTH enters a bar. BESS is playing Big Buck Hunter, already shooting, by herself, at the Buck Hunter machine. RUTH approaches. RUTH watches BESS.)*

BESS: You want to play?

RUTH: Um…sure. It looks—

BESS: It's great. It is my favorite thing.

RUTH: It looks great.

BESS: It's great. Have you played before?

RUTH: Uh-uh.

BESS: Don't worry. It's easy to learn.

RUTH: You just shoot the deer?

BESS: They're buck.

RUTH: What do you mean?

BESS: They're not deer. They're buck.

RUTH: Oh. I'm sorry. I thought—

BESS: Sure. Everyone does.

(BESS *hands* RUTH *the gun.*)

BESS: Now. Take your stance. That's the most important part. A good stance. It's your connection to power.

RUTH: Okay. *(She takes a stance.)*

BESS: No. You need your weight distributed like— See? Spread your legs a little. Like Tai Chi. Good. Now. Take aim.

(RUTH *takes aim.*)

BESS: Cock the gun. Shoot.

(RUTH *shoots.*)

RUTH: Wow.

BESS: I know, right?

RUTH: Oh my God. Wow.

BESS: I'm addicted.

RUTH: This is going to change my life entirely.

BESS: It will.

RUTH: I needed this.

BESS: I can tell.

RUTH: You can? How can you tell?

BESS: You're tense and freaked out. This will steady you.

(BESS *and* RUTH *put money into the machine, and* BESS *prepares to shoot.*)

BESS: We'll start in Canada.

RUTH: Great. I love snow.

BESS: I love this game.

RUTH: Me too. It's amazing.

BESS: Exhilarating.

RUTH: Thrilling.

BESS: Sexy

RUTH: Totally sexy.

BESS: It makes me feel hot. Like a guy.

RUTH: It's the stance.

BESS: I told you. And the whiskey.

RUTH: Wow.

BESS: And it's good to be the person who shoots. Not the one getting shot at. The active. Not the passive. The hunter. Not the animal.

RUTH: I love sound they make when they die.

BESS: The thud.

RUTH: Yes. The thud. It's—

BESS: Satisfying.

RUTH: Yes.

BESS: I hate my boyfriend.

RUTH: Really?

BESS: He's out of town. And shooting buck totally helps. Takes away the edge. I can pretend the target is him. I put his face on the animals. The big dumb ones.

RUTH: What's he doing out of town?

BESS: Running away.

RUTH: From you?

BESS: From everything.

RUTH: That sucks.

BESS: Yes.

(BESS and RUTH shoot.)

BESS: You know, men don't know they want to be in relationships until you prove to them that this is false. I mean, they say they want to be alone. But that's a lie. What they *want* is to feel trapped. They like to complain about it. Feeling trapped, tricked, controlled. But they want it. They totally do.

RUTH: That's my problem. I never did that, trap them.

BESS: It's the only way. It's like they want to know that they were not the person responsible for making the relationship happen so that they can't blame themselves if and when they have to go. They like to feel that the woman tricked them. They like to feel controlled.

RUTH: I think you're right.

BESS: I don't mind. I'm a great girlfriend. It's a talent of mine. I was raised to be a great girlfriend. I don't mind standing in the background because I'm holding all the cards.

RUTH: You're amazing. I can't do that.

BESS: Can't do what?

RUTH: Any of it. I can't do any of it.

BESS: Not true. You can shoot.

RUTH: Sure. But I can't trap.

BESS: Yeah. But you can work on that. Develop your skills. Practice. It's just like shooting.

RUTH: Really?

BESS: Sure.

(BESS *and* RUTH *take a break.*)

RUTH: You know how love changes you?

BESS: No.

RUTH: No?

BESS: No.

RUTH: Oh. Well. It does. At least it changes *me*. Burns stuff. Knocks it out. Wipes it clean. Levels everything. It does—it changes you. Leaves you altered.

BESS: That sounds awful.

RUTH: No. It's really nice. It's the best part. You get altered, and then Love goes away, and you just have to readjust or something.

BESS: What's the point of that?

RUTH: What's the point of anything?

BESS: I don't know.

RUTH: It's the best thing human beings do.

BESS: Your generation has the strangest ideas about love.

(RUTH *says nothing.*)

BESS: Look at the animal kingdom. The animal kingdom has lessons for us. Messages. Division of labor.

RUTH: But what if I don't want to lay traps? What if I want someone to come to me of his own free will?

BESS: Yeah, good luck with that.

RUTH: But—

BESS: It just doesn't work. The point is not to be "altered" —that's just lame-ass therapy language. The point is to find someone to be with, to make a commitment, to have families and ensure the survival of our way of life. And take a vacation here and there to cool places.

RUTH: But—

BESS: Look. I know you're older than me and you've probably had a lot of really important life experiences and all, but—you're single. And I know. I study these things. I have had a subscription to Cosmopolitan since I was twelve. And between that and the works of the Western literary canon, I mean, come on. Get real. It doesn't happen the way you're saying. You can be a predator or prey. You can be a wolf or a bunny rabbit. And bunny rabbits don't survive. Do they?

RUTH: Maybe you're right.

BESS: I'm right. Trust me. I'm like twenty, and I am prepared for anything. How about the Midwest? Want to shoot there? It's harder than Canada.

(BESS *puts more bills in the machine.* RUTH *watches, mesmerized.*)

BESS: Do you come here a lot?

(RUTH *nods. Then:*)

RUTH: No. I've never been here before.

BESS: Well, my girlfriends from school and I come here all the time to shoot. So if you want to do this again, we're usually here Monday and Tuesday nights; Tonight's an anomaly because I'm emotionally volatile. (*Note: she does not seem the slightest bit emotionally volatile*) I think this game will help you.

RUTH: Help me? Help me what?

BESS: Survive.

*(Scene: Late night at* JESSE's. ASTOR *sits on the couch not waiting for Ruth.* RUTH *enters. She is surprised to see him. And maybe a little drunk)*

RUTH: Oh!

ASTOR: I can't sleep. I was not waiting up.

RUTH: What do you think about survival?

ASTOR: Uh—? In what sense?

*(*RUTH *sits next to* ASTOR.*)*

RUTH: I met this girl in a bar uptown.

ASTOR: Uptown?

RUTH: I walked. We shot Buck.

ASTOR: What does that mean?

RUTH: It's a video game. The girl said men want to be trapped.

ASTOR: That's kind of true.

RUTH: That SUCKS.

ASTOR: I don't.

RUTH: The girl said a bunch of stuff about division of labor and the Western European canon and self-preservation. I love this girl. And Big Buck Hunter is going to change my life. Thanks to her.
Have you ever played?

ASTOR: I'm a purist with video games. Old school. Ms Pac Man. Centipede.

RUTH: You're not old enough to be old school.

ASTOR: Killing goes against my Buddha nature.

RUTH: You kill in Ms Pac Man. It's cannibalism.

ASTOR: It's different. The noises are different.

RUTH: These noises are hot.

ASTOR: Hot?

RUTH: You know, in packs of animals which are dominated by an "alpha male" power is disseminated according to male attributes. Anything that makes you look like a female is considered a sign of weakness. And they are unforgiving to the weak. They rip your heart out; they rip it right out.

ASTOR: I don't.

RUTH: Tonight, when I held the gun—

ASTOR: You held a gun?

RUTH: That's what I'm telling you! It was orange and plastic. And when I held it, something happened.

ASTOR: What happened?

RUTH: I'm never going back.

ASTOR: I'm not unforgiving to females.

RUTH: You're not a predator.

ASTOR: You're not a predator.

RUTH: But I could become one.

ASTOR: Honey.

RUTH: I don't want to go back to being the person who gets killed. Maimed. Rendered homeless and heartbroken. I'm never going to be that person again.

ASTOR: Okay, Killer. No one wants you to be that person.

RUTH: Good. Because I'm not going to be her.

ASTOR: Okay. (Beat) Want a glass of water?

RUTH: No. Want to play shooting games online?

ASTOR: No. Want to watch weird old movies?

RUTH: No. Want to surf craigslist and look for our next apartment?

ASTOR: No. Want to make out?

RUTH: No. *(She gets off the couch.)*

ASTOR: Just asking.

RUTH: Why?

ASTOR: I don't know. Because.

RUTH: Well. No.

ASTOR: Okay.

RUTH: Shit.

ASTOR: Don't freak out or anything.

RUTH: I'm not freaking out. Where's my sweater?

ASTOR: I don't know, over there.

*(RUTH goes to cover herself with a big sweater. Moves to the other side of the room)*

ASTOR: It was just a thought.

RUTH: Okay. Sure.

ASTOR: I mean, you're like, ready to make a home with some guy in Queens who you barely know—

RUTH: I read his books!

ASTOR: So!? I mean, we're already home to each other, and who cares what it looks like or means. It is the opposite of a trap. And we're—I mean, I just thought, it's a risk, but—!? Forget it.

RUTH: Sure! I mean, no— But—I mean—

ASTOR: What? You mean what!?

RUTH: I don't know!

ASTOR: If you mention my age or my brother I swear to God I will stop being your friend right now. Things like this happen all the time!

RUTH: No. They don't.

ASTOR: Sure they do. Haven't you seen *Moonstruck*?

RUTH: But I'm— you know—I don't—I don't even know what I want, or what's best, or how to know what's best or anything, I don't even KNOW.

ASTOR: So?

RUTH: So, I don't know. I don't know. I mean, I don't know.

ASTOR: You don't scare me. And I don't need to be trapped. *(Beat)*
Look, forget it. I just thought—it was an impulse, okay? Just like, a thought—something to do—and— I'm not in love with you. I just—love you. You're my friend. And I thought it might be a cool risk. Like the kind of cool risk that— But don't go getting all freaked in this major way if it's—a problem for your survival!

*(The phone rings. ASTOR and RUTH both stare.)*

ASTOR: Don't answer it.

RUTH: Why?

ASTOR: I don't know.

*(They don't answer it. They regard the phone as if monsters will leap out. The archaic analog answering machine picks up, and BESS leaves a message.)*

*(BESS's voice:)*

BESS: Hey. It's me. Are you checking messages from out there? I'm going to get you a cell phone when you get back to the City. Just admit you miss me, okay? Admit it. Anyway. I'm at a party. *(Yelling to someone in the background:)* YEAH I'LL BE RIGHT THERE. They're taking their clothes off in the commons room, Lucy is wasted. But, I miss you. You miss me? I miss you…

*(RUTH and ASTOR stare.)*

RUTH: Who was *that*!?

ASTOR: Wrong number?

RUTH: Is he, is he seeing someone? Someone with a "commons room"?

ASTOR: I don't know.

RUTH: Ohhh. I should go.

ASTOR: Where?

RUTH: I DON'T KNOW. I DO NOT KNOW WHERE! OKAY!?

ASTOR: You don't have to.

RUTH: I do.

ASTOR: I don't want you to.

RUTH: Tough.

ASTOR: Listen—

RUTH: It's fine. Really. Good. This is all good—I'm good— Oh fuck. *(She starts to cry—torrentially. In one gulp)* It's just that I'm not a predator. I'm not a big buck hunter. I'm a bunny rabbit. A pathetic, little furry tailed bunny fucking rabbit. I am prey. I don't know how to lay traps. I am unskilled and unqualified to live in this world. And I will die by the side of the road. Like the bunny rabbit corpse I am. I gotta go. *(She goes to leave—then, at the last moment, turns back around, goes to him, kisses him.)* I think this is wrong.

ASTOR: Okay.

*(ASTOR kisses RUTH back. They start for the bedroom then remember it is JESSE's. So instead, they settle wherever it makes sense for them to do so—and then—eros.)*

*(Blackout)*

*(Scene: JESSE addresses the audience from the front seat of the van.)*

JESSE: So anyway. You decide you're going to go. Drive. And you do. You map-quest the route. Mapquest. I wish I could Mapquest my life. And you have your map and you get into the van and you fill up with gas and you fasten your seatbelts. You go. You do not take the turn to Elizabeth New Jersey IKEA. You go North. Through upstate New York and into Vermont and you keep going, through mountains and past the Ben and Jerry's ice cream outlet, past Burlington where the University of Vermont—which is a really good state school—lies, and across the border and you might get all the way to Montreal where the people speak another language entirely, and you can lose yourself there, you really can, only you can't. All the pieces you've already lost start to come back to you. Maybe it's the snow. But… It all starts coming back. Fuck.

*(Scene: Clarity at the Howard Johnsons)*

RUTH: *(First, an aside)* Yeah I didn't know they had one of these in New York City either. But they do. They have two. *(Then, back in scene…she picks up the phone)* Room service?
Can you send up—?
Oh you don't have room service, eh?
Bare bones, right?
Got it.
You have a knish place downstairs and an all-night deli, and that should be good enough.
Well, you're right it is (for the record, you have phones up here with buttons that say "room service" —It's true.)
But can I ask you something, Room Service?
Can you talk for a minute?
Can I just tell you—?
I was in my ex-lover's apartment yesterday, last night, and can I just tell you,
I have no idea who he is.

At the time, I mean, during the actual affair, I did
I think I did.
I think it was a very important affair like in Graham
Green novels,
I think it opened all these many things—
It was one of those deep affairs, the kind that burns
everything in its path, you know?
Right. Like that.
Sometimes I'd find myself standing in the middle of
the room
Unable to figure out where I was going
But anyway
Now, after the fact,
after we've both moved
(I mean, literally moved)
I moved on.
And, I didn't know it until last night.
Well really until I slept with his brother who is, or was,
my best friend.
Which is a very strange concept, I mean a strange
thing to pretend to have, a Best Friend, when you're
over thirty. It's not only a bad label because it makes
you sound like a twelve year old girl but also, it's
unrealistic.
Grown-ups don't get to have "best friends".
Maybe because we fuck them and ruin it.
Maybe for other reasons, I don't know.
The world is a very strange place.
Do you want to go to the all-night deli with me
and look at magazines and buy some cashews or
something?
Oh really?
What time does your shift end?
There's this video game I like to play—
No seriously hear me out.
It'll change your life.
I promise.

*(Scene:* JESSE *comes home.)*

JESSE: Thanks for looking after the place.

ASTOR: No problem.

JESSE: Anything happen?

ASTOR: What do you mean?

JESSE: While I was gone?

ASTOR: Like what?

JESSE: Um, like—I don't know. Pipes burst? Landlord call? Meet Hot Coke-Mom-Neighbor upstairs? Hot water get, um, whatever it is, you know when the hot water…?

ASTOR: Nothing happened.

JESSE: Do you want to stay?

ASTOR: With you?

JESSE: With me. You shouldn't be unstable like this. You shouldn't be here and there and on all those couches, not when you have family. You should just stay with me. We can turn the office back into a second bedroom.

ASTOR: No.

JESSE: No?

ASTOR: No.

JESSE: But why?

ASTOR: It isn't what I want.

JESSE: Oh. But—

ASTOR: It's a very generous offer. But no.

*(Beat)*

JESSE: This whole thing is hard.

ASTOR: What part of it?

JESSE: All of it. I don't always know how to be a good brother. I'm sorry.

ASTOR: You're doing fine.

JESSE: Driving is strange. And healing. Is that the van?

ASTOR: That's the van.

JESSE: Pieces are starting to come back.

ASTOR: What kind of pieces?

JESSE: The way Deirdre used to smile. And how it felt when she stopped. The day I met Ruth. How she said we would not have an affair, and then, how we had an affair. How hot it was that summer. There was a heat wave and Ruth didn't believe in air conditioning. In New York City!

ASTOR: She got past that.

JESSE: Good. She was so different than Deirdre.

ASTOR: Warmer.

JESSE: Yes. The last day we were together, right before the end, she stood across the street, watching me go—only I couldn't go while she was watching, and I was late. And I had to go, but didn't. We both just stood there. Watching each other not move…I keep remembering things I hoped were gone. But they're not gone.

*(This is painful for* ASTOR.*)*

ASTOR: I have to go I have to. I'm sorry.

JESSE: Oh.

ASTOR: No. Look. It isn't you. I'll call you. This is good. *(Beat)* If you talk to Mom, tell her I'm back in Inwood.

JESSE: Hey!

ASTOR: What?

*(*JESSE *tosses* ASTOR *the keys.)*

ASTOR: Thanks.

(ASTOR *goes.* JESSE *is left alone.*)

(*Scene*)

BESS: Did you have some kind of melt-down in Canada?

JESSE: I started remembering things.

BESS: What kind of things?

JESSE: Just. Things. Dumb things. Little things. Details.

BESS: It's okay. We can slow down. I met someone while you were away anyhow. And, like, he's my age. So that's cool. I don't have to like—try so hard, you know, to act old. Or make up for past damage. So lets slow down. And in the meantime, I might date Jorge a little bit and like, we'll just see what happens.

JESSE: Jorge? Who's Jorge?

BESS: No one. Just this guy my age. We're in the same Poly-Sci section.

JESSE: What Poly Sci section?

BESS: I take that survey Poly-Sci class twice a week. Tuesdays and Thursdays.

JESSE: I didn't know that.

BESS: There's a lot you don't know.

JESSE: Clearly.

BESS: Are you okay?

JESSE: I don't know.

BESS: I missed you. Want to make out for old times sake? Old times with me, not the ones you're like flooded with or whatever. Besides, I don't care about your past. I'm all about right now.

JESSE: That's true. You are.

BESS: Take me home.

(JESSE *does.*)

*(Scene)*

ASTOR: Is it Jesse?

RUTH: It's a lot of things.

ASTOR: So talk about them!

RUTH: I'm not sure where to start.

ASTOR: Wherever, Dude.

RUTH: Don't call me Dude. We had sex. When you have sex with a woman, you can't call her "Dude." EVER AGAIN.

ASTOR: Fine. Ruth.

RUTH: I don't like that either. Ruth.

ASTOR: *(Losing patience)* What do you like then?

RUTH: I don't know. *(Beat)* It wasn't THIS all along, was it? Has it always been this, and I just didn't know?

ASTOR: I don't know.

RUTH: I don't want it to be this.

ASTOR: Is that why you haven't been calling?

RUTH: *(Changing the subject)* You want to shoot buck?

ASTOR: No.

RUTH: Are you sure? It takes the edge off.

ASTOR: What edge?

RUTH: This one.

ASTOR: The girl I'm friends with doesn't shoot animals.

RUTH: They're not real animals.

ASTOR: She doesn't shoot fake animals.

RUTH: The girl you're friends with has not been taking very good care of herself. Or haven't you noticed?

She's made random choices based on some fantasy of how the world works, and it's not exactly serving her. The girl you're friends with—

ASTOR: Yes?

RUTH: —needs to get real.

ASTOR: That's too bad. I liked her the way she was. Unreal. Heart open. Expecting the best.

RUTH: I don't want to see you for awhile.

ASTOR: Fine by me. *(He leaves.)*

*(Scene:* RUTH *in the rain.)*

RUTH: Stalking the apartment. I see the apartment. I have identified and looked at it. I have turned in an application. And now, using the Buck Hunter stance, I stand across the street, every night until they decide. Watching to see what happens, who comes and goes, whether they look nice, whether it feels safe and whether or not this is a place I could belong. I ask, do I feel at home? In the presence of the building, do I feel any instinctual clue? A "homing" device? Can I place my energy into the building from across the street and start to bond with it even before the paperwork has gone through? And then, based on this energetic bond, will the landlord be persuaded to ignore my tax returns and the word "self employed" and pay attention instead to the subtle way in which I already belong in his building?
I pretend to be the girl in the dive bar. The one who moves through life as if it's a straight line. The one who can keep her eye on the target and pursue what she wants without fear. For that girl, there is no ambivalence. No theory. No gray area. Just black. And white. A clear path home.

*(Scene: A café. Weeks later. Something in this scene is in relief, to the rest of the play, as if this is the scene we've*

*been waiting for all along and its visual rules are different somehow.)*

RUTH: I was surprised. To hear from you.

JESSE: How are you?

RUTH: Good.

JESSE: Good.

RUTH: Good.

JESSE: What are you doing? I mean, what are you up to?

RUTH: Not much. *(Beat, then brightly, oversharing again:)* I've lived in six apartments and had about four jobs in the last year, all of them in some form of education or social services. I have made transience into an art project. Which just means I kept a journal and shot a roll of film in each place. I learned about survival. I stopped visiting places we used to go together. I stopped waiting for you to find me. I read a lot of Eastern European novels about memory and lightness and weight. And mostly I've just been living my life. You?

JESSE: The same.

*(Beat)*

JESSE: Astor said—

RUTH: Yes?

JESSE: That you were in Queens.

RUTH: Oh. No. I'm in the City now.

JESSE: Another sublet?

RUTH: No. A real lease. In my name. Two years. I have this friend who works at the Howard Johnson on Houston and her uncle is the super of this building, so…I move in on Tuesday.

JESSE: I have a new place too. It has these, it's old, and it has all those moldings and great floors.

RUTH: I know. I mean, I see.

JESSE: It's in Gramercy. Like a Wharton novel. Like *The Age of Innocence.*

RUTH: I lived there once. A long time ago. Gramercy, not *The Age of Innocence.*

JESSE: If you join the synagogue, they give you a key to the park.

RUTH: Really?

JESSE: Yes.

RUTH: Did you? Join? For the key to the—?

JESSE: No. *(Beat)* Are you—?

RUTH: Joining a synagogue for a key to a park?

JESSE: No, I don't know. Just—I don't know. Are you well? Are you good?

RUTH: Yes. I am.

JESSE: Good. Me too. You know just—

RUTH: Yes?

JESSE: No. Nothing.

RUTH: It was. Just like you said. A beginning

JESSE: What do you mean?

RUTH: You called it a beginning. With us.

JESSE: I don't remember.

RUTH: You don't?

*(JESSE doesn't answer.)*

RUTH: Oh. Well. You said, "I need you to know this is a beginning."

JESSE: *(I remember.)*

RUTH: And it was. Just not the kind we thought.

JESSE: It's good to see you.

(JESSE *tries to take* RUTH's *hand, and she doesn't know how to respond. It's as if, instinctually, she wants to take his back, but then, also instinctually, can't. An awkward dance of hands. This is probably the first time that they have been together with all of their respective clothing on since initially meeting. They smile, nervously.*)

RUTH: I should go.

JESSE: Do you have to?

RUTH: Yes. *(Beat)* Hey. Thank you.

JESSE: For what?

RUTH: Everything.

JESSE: I don't know what you mean.

RUTH: Well. Thank you for the beginning. And the, the way you opened something in me and then—left it there, open. Which was good. I didn't know it, but it was good. Thank you for opening me and leaving me alone with the opening so I could find it all without you. Thank you for showing me how to love. Thank you for helping me to get to the next moment of life and for un-sticking me from any of the things I thought I'd be stuck to. Thank you for getting inside of me, my body and heart, in this way that just really mattered. Thank you for that. And for forcing me to move on. When all was said and done, thank you for forcing me to move on. Thank you for helping me not want you anymore.

(JESSE *and* RUTH *hold one another's gaze. Beat*)

JESSE: Oh. You're welcome. I guess. *(Beat)* So—?

RUTH: No. That's all.

JESSE: That's all what?

RUTH: I have to go.

JESSE: But—?

RUTH: I have to go home. *(She leaves.)*

*(Scene: Home)*

*(*RUTH *drags her boxes across the floor and into her "home".)*

*(Scene:* ASTOR *joins* RUTH *in her home.)*

ASTOR: You moved in without me.

RUTH: I did.

ASTOR: I had the van.

RUTH: I know.

ASTOR: I would have helped.

RUTH: I know.

ASTOR: But you had to do it on your own.

RUTH: I did. *(Beat)* I was waiting.

ASTOR: For?

RUTH: First, I was waiting to find a place. Then I was waiting to get settled. Then, I was waiting have something decent to say. To you. Some kind of, I don't know, clarity? Vision? Only I haven't had any kind of, anything, to say. And then I just missed you. So. I called.

*(This is awkward. Neither knows how to begin.)*

ASTOR: I'm glad you called.

RUTH: I don't know who we are to each other.

ASTOR: I don't know either. "Who we are." "To each other." I'm a Buddhist, so I don't even believe we have selves, which sort of complicates this whole notion of "Who We Are"…

RUTH: I get it.

ASTOR: But it's not like you said. It's not like there was an agenda.

RUTH: I know.

*(Beat)*

ASTOR: The apartment is nice.

RUTH: It is, right?

ASTOR: You get the stuff from storage?

RUTH: Not yet.

ASTOR: "Waiting" on that too? *(He takes a sip of tea, grimaces.)* What is this? It tastes like a twig.

RUTH: It's Kukicha tea. It is a twig.

ASTOR: Want to go to the Shore?

RUTH: Right now?

ASTOR: This entire conversation would be so much better if we were driving to The Shore. Watching things move. Come on. What else are you doing?

RUTH: Unpacking?

ASTOR: You have no stuff.

RUTH: True.

ASTOR: Come on. The Shore. Like in Springsteen songs.

RUTH: Which ones?

ASTOR: Like, most of them.

RUTH: Oh. Yeah. Well. *(Beat, awkwardly)* So we just, keep going?

ASTOR: Yeah. Like people who love each other. We feel it out. Make mistakes. Keep going.

RUTH: I can do that.

ASTOR: Good. Me too.

RUTH: The Shore.

ASTOR: They have an arcade.

(RUTH *lights up.*)

RUTH: Buck Hunter?

ASTOR: Dance Dance Revolution.

RUTH: Not the same thing.

ASTOR: For you maybe. For me, Dance Dance Revolution. Come on. You'll love it. No one gets hurt. Music. No guns.

RUTH: I like the van.

ASTOR: Chicks do.

RUTH: And it would be nice. To see the ocean.

ASTOR: We can swing by the storage space on the way home.

RUTH: We can?

ASTOR: Oh yeah. With the van, all things are possible.

RUTH: Well. Okay. *(She starts to get her stuff.)* Will you let me drive?

ASTOR: No.

RUTH: That's okay. I don't really want to. *(She gets a bag, her keys, looks around her apartment…)* How long do you think it will last?

ASTOR: The place?

(RUTH *nods.*)

ASTOR: Who knows? Come on. The shore awaits.

*(As* ASTOR *and* RUTH *head for the door)*

RUTH: Are you still in Inwood?

ASTOR: Not only am I there, but I am now paying "rent". I even have my own "room".

RUTH: Wow.

ASTOR: I know. I'm like the unofficial Super. I'm the only guy who knows how everything works.

RUTH: I am impressed.

(RUTH *turns out the light. They leave, closing the door— from offstage:)*

RUTH: Oh! I have to do something. *(She opens the door again, turns on the light, looks one more time at her home, looks around, then smiles. Big smile.)* Even if it doesn't last. Thank you. *(She turns out the light again—closes the door— and goes.)*

END OF PLAY